InterActions
small group series

Practical
Steps for
Spiritual
Growth

ESSENTIAL
CHRISTIANITY

Interactions Small Group Series

InterActions
small group series

Practical
Steps for
Spiritual
Growth

ESSENTIAL
CHRISTIANITY

BILL HYBELS

WITH KEVIN AND SHERRY HARNEY

ZONDERVAN®

WILLOW
Willow Creek Resources

ZONDERVAN.com/
AUTHORTRACKER
follow your favorite authors

ZONDERVAN®

Essential Christianity
Copyright © 1998 by Willow Creek Association

Requests for information should be addressed to:

Zondervan, *Grand Rapids, Michigan* 49530

ISBN 978-0-310-26604-4

Interior design by Rick Devon & Michelle Espinoza

Printed in the United States of America

08 09 10 11 12 13 14 • 23 22 21 20 19 18 17 16 15 14 13 12 11 10 9 8 7 6 5

CONTENTS

INTERACTIONS

In 1992, Willow Creek Community Church, in partnership with Zondervan and the Willow Creek Association, released a curriculum for small groups entitled the Walking with God series. In just three years, almost a half million copies of these small group study guides were being used in churches around the world. The phenomenal response to this curriculum affirmed the need for relevant and biblical small group materials.

At the writing of this curriculum, there were nearly 3,000 small groups meeting regularly within the structure of Willow Creek Community Church. We believe this number will increase as we continue to place a central value on small groups. Many other churches throughout the world are growing in their commitment to small group ministries as well, so the need for resources is increasing.

In response to this great need, the Interactions small group series has been developed. Willow Creek Association and Zondervan have joined together to create a whole new approach to small group materials. These discussion guides are meant to challenge group members to a deeper level of sharing, create lines of accountability, move followers of Christ into action, and help group members become fully devoted followers of Christ.

SUGGESTIONS FOR INDIVIDUAL STUDY

1. Begin each session with prayer. Ask God to help you understand the passage and to apply it to your life.
2. A good modern translation, such as the New International Version, the New American Standard Bible, or the New Revised Standard Version, will give you the most help. Questions in this guide are based on the New International Version.
3. Read and reread the passage(s). You must know what the passage says before you can understand what it means and how it applies to you.
4. Write your answers in the spaces provided in the study guide. This will help you to express clearly your understanding of the passage.
5. Keep a Bible dictionary handy. Use it to look up unfamiliar words, names, or places.

SUGGESTIONS FOR GROUP STUDY

1. Come to the session prepared. Careful preparation will greatly enrich your time in group discussion.
2. Be willing to join in the discussion. The leader of the group will not be lecturing but will encourage people to discuss what they have learned in the passage. Plan to share what God has taught you in your individual study.
3. Stick to the passage being studied. Base your answers on the verses being discussed rather than on outside authorities such as commentaries or your favorite author or speaker.
4. Try to be sensitive to the other members of the group. Listen attentively when they speak, and be affirming whenever you can. This will encourage more hesitant members of the group to participate.
5. Be careful not to dominate the discussion. By all means participate, but allow others to have equal time.
6. If you are the discussion leader, you will find additional suggestions and helpful ideas in the Leader's Notes.

ADDITIONAL RESOURCES AND TEACHING MATERIALS

At the end of this study guide you will find a collection of resources and teaching materials to help you in your growth as a follower of Christ. You will also find resources that will help your church develop and build fully devoted followers of Christ.

Introduction: Practical Steps for Spiritual Growth

Almost every week I stand before thousands of people at Willow Creek Community Church and seek to teach God's truth in a clear and relevant manner. As I look out at the many faces, it occurs to me that there are four categories of people that make up the Willow Creek congregation, and almost every church gathering across the face of the earth.

First, gathered each week are people who are truly Christian. Biblically defined, they are people who have met Jesus Christ in a personal way. He has become their forgiver and the leader of their life. They have a living and dynamic relationship with God and are fully devoted followers of Christ. They live with a quiet assurance that by God's grace, through the work of Jesus Christ on the cross, their sins have been forgiven.

The second category consists of people who think they are Christians but who, in reality, are not. These people remind me of someone sitting at a departure gate in an airport, ticket gripped firmly in fist. Everyone in the waiting area is planning on getting on a plane in just a few moments; however, one of these people has no idea that the ticket he purchased at a "super-saver fare" from Mr. Cheapo Travel Service is bogus—he was sold a counterfeit ticket. In the same way, many people sitting in churches every weekend think they are Christians. They may even be fairly sure about it, but they shouldn't be! Their assurance is based on false premises. They are holding a bogus ticket.

The third group are those people who are Christians but who do not live with the confidence and assurance the Bible says they should have. They are like the people in the waiting area at an airport who have a legitimate ticket but who still fear that the plane is going to leave without them. Their fear appears irrational to us, but to them it is a debilitating reality.

Finally, there is a fourth group of people in every church. These are people who are not followers of Christ. They come to find out what God's Word says about how to become a Christian. They come investigating, seeking, and searching.

Week by week they discover another piece of the spiritual puzzle and put it in its place. Over time they begin to see a clear, compelling picture of what it takes to become a Christ follower.

This series of six studies is designed to address the most important issues a human being will ever face. How does a person become a follower of Christ? How does a person live with assurance of their eternal destiny? How can a follower of Christ live a radically committed life of growth and maturity in faith? How can we effectively tell others about Jesus? The goal of this study is to present God's truth with clarity and power and to strip away the false assurances to which some may be clinging. I want to go around the waiting area and say to all the people, "Let's look at your ticket. If you are carrying a bogus ticket, it is time to find out how you can get a real one."

Bill Hybels

KNOWING CHRIST

THE BIG PICTURE

Have you ever wondered what you might say to the people you love if you knew you had only one more chance to communicate with them? What would you say? What would you want to communicate?

If I knew I could write only one more book, teach only one more class, preach only one more message, or write only one more small group study guide, it would be on the topics contained in the following pages. I am referring to the absolute basics. Not basics in terms of simplistic thoughts or truths, but basics in terms of the core building blocks of life.

It is not difficult for me to get motivated to prepare messages on a whole variety of subjects. I love to teach on themes that traverse the landscape of human experience. Over the years I have tackled topics such as Christians in the marketplace, Christians in a sex-crazed culture, handling personal finances, and developing healthy relationships. I have been privileged to give messages on many books of the Bible and speak on a vast array of themes and topics. But of all of these, none is more important than what we will focus on in this study.

From time to time we need to strip away all the extraneous material and get right to the heart of the Christian message. This core message of the Christian faith has transformed my life. It grips me every time I have an opportunity to communicate it. Whether I am talking with one person over a cup of coffee, leading a small group, or teaching a few thousand people, it really doesn't make any difference—it is the same life-changing message every time.

A WIDE ANGLE VIEW

1 If you knew it was your last chance to speak your heart, what would you say to a family member or friend who was not a Christ follower?

A BIBLICAL PORTRAIT

Read Genesis 3:1–21

2 After Adam and Eve ate the fruit and disobeyed God, the way they looked at everything changed. What shift occurred in the way they viewed *one* of the following:

- How they viewed themselves
- How they viewed each other
- How they viewed their God

3

Adam and Eve saw God slaughter innocent animals so that He could make clothing to cover their nakedness and shame. What did Adam and Eve learn about *one* of the following:

- Their condition
- God's view of sin
- The price of sin

SHARPENING THE FOCUS

Read Snapshot "The Passover Lamb"

THE PASSOVER LAMB

God had told Moses that every Israelite family must sacrifice a lamb and place the blood of that lamb on the doorpost of their home. If they would not, the firstborn male of their home would die when the angel of death came over Egypt.

Imagine you are transported back in time to Egypt in the days of Moses. You are in a pasture as a Jewish father is taking his twelve-year-old son out to find a one-year-old lamb.

"What are we doing, Dad?" the boy asks.

"We are going to get a prize sheep."

"What for, Dad?"

"You will see."

They find the best lamb in the flock and bring it back to the shed. The boy sees his dad get the machete. "What are you going to do, Dad?" the boy asks again.

"I am going to slaughter the lamb."

"What did the lamb do, Dad?"

The father thinks long and hard and tries to form his words very carefully. "Son, the lamb didn't do anything, but our nation has sinned against God. He is about ready to exercise justice and pass judgment on all of us. But God said that if we find an innocent third party, an innocent unblemished lamb, the lamb's blood will act as a covering for us."

The son thinks about this and says, "Dad, that sounds very unfair. What happens if we don't sacrifice the lamb?"

With a solemn look at his son, the father speaks the truth. "If we don't sacrifice the lamb and place its blood on the doorpost of our house, you will die before morning."

---

4 If you were that son talking to his father, what would you say to your dad at this point in the conversation?

How would you feel if you were the son?

5 If you were the father, how would you explain the necessity of the lamb being sacrificed?

Read Snapshot "A Perfect Sacrifice Is Coming"

A PERFECT SACRIFICE IS COMING

More than 700 years B.C. the prophet Isaiah broadcast a news brief that spread across the land. Isaiah started talking about a new sacrifice, an ultimate sacrifice, the final sacrifice. He said that an innocent third party would once again pay the price for sinful people. But this time the sacrifice would be radically different; it would not be a lamb, but an innocent human (see Isa. 53:1–7). Centuries before it would happen, Isaiah pointed to a perfect sacrifice that would be paid to free people from their sins and save them from judgment.

Now turn the clock ahead to the first century. Jesus has already been born and is about thirty years old. A man by the name of John the Baptist is living in the desert outside of Jerusalem. Multitudes of people are coming out to hear him preach and be baptized. One day, in front of all of the people, John catches a glimpse of Jesus. John hushes the crowd and says, "Look, the Lamb of God, who takes away the sin of the world!" (John 1:29). John is declaring the truth. Jesus is the ultimate Lamb, the innocent third party who will shed His blood as the payment for sinful people.

6 Isaiah pointed to Jesus and wrote:

He was despised and rejected by men, a man of sorrows, and familiar with suffering. Like one from whom men hide their faces he was despised, and we esteemed him not. Surely he took up our infirmities and carried our sorrows, yet we considered him stricken by God, smitten by him, and afflicted. But he was pierced for our transgressions, he was crushed for our iniquities; the punishment that brought us peace was upon him, and by his wounds we are healed. We all, like sheep, have gone astray, each of us has turned to his own way; and the LORD has laid on him the iniquity of us all.

ISAIAH 53:3–6

What did Isaiah promise that Jesus would do for you?

How do you feel when you read these words?

7 Think about the story of the father and son going out to find a prize lamb to sacrifice so they could place its blood on the doorpost of their home as a covering. What did Jesus have in common with the sacrificial lamb of Exodus?

Read Snapshot "Jesus, the Final Sacrifice"

JESUS, THE FINAL SACRIFICE

 It is the first century, and you are in the grandstands right outside of the court of Pontius Pilate. Jesus has been arrested. He is convicted on false charges and now, as He is strapped up, a Roman soldier takes a whip with nine straps covered with pieces of metal and glass and begins flogging Jesus in public. You see the blood of the sinless, only begotten Son of God begin to flow. You watch as Jesus is brought to the hill of Calvary where an executioner gets delight in pounding nails into His wrists and feet. The blood of the perfect Lamb of God continues to flow.

You remember that Jesus said to His followers that nobody could take His life. You realize this is no accident—Jesus is laying down His life for your sins. An innocent third party is paying the price you deserve. As you look at Him on the cross, you realize His blood is flowing so that your blood won't have to flow.

As the last drops of His life blood are flowing onto the dusty ground at the foot of the cross, you hear Jesus cry out "It is finished." You realize this is not a cry of defeat but a declaration of victory! Finally, all sacrifices are now over. The ultimate sacrifice has come—it has been paid with the blood of Jesus. Through Christ our sins have been paid in full. As you watch Him die, you know you are loved beyond measure and description. You realize that God has exercised His judgment on His own precious Son, and He is not angry with you anymore. Through accepting Christ as your Savior, His blood is applied to the door of your heart and judgment passes over you.

---

8 If you have received God's forgiveness through the shed blood of Christ, describe when this happened and how it has changed your life.

If you have not yet received this forgiveness, what is standing in the way?

9 Knowing the price God paid to show His love for you and realizing what Jesus did to offer you forgiveness, what words of thanks and praise do you want to lift to God?

PUTTING YOURSELF IN THE PICTURE

REMEMBER, REMEMBER, REMEMBER

May we never forget the price God paid to offer us forgiveness of sins. Take time in the coming week to memorize Isaiah 53:5–6. Think deeply about them and remember the depth of God's love for you.

> But he was pierced for our transgressions, he was crushed for our iniquities; the punishment that brought us peace was upon him, and by his wounds we are healed. We all, like sheep, have gone astray, each of us has turned to his own way; and the LORD has laid on him the iniquity of us all.

MAKING AN IMPACT LIST

If you have received God's forgiveness through Christ, you will want others to know God's love. Make a list of some people in your life who are not followers of Christ. Commit yourself to praying for them regularly during the time you are part of this small group study. Also, pray for God to open doors of opportunity for you to begin talking to others about your love for Jesus.

- _____

- _____

- _____

- _____

- _____

LIVING WITH ASSURANCE

REFLECTIONS FROM SESSION 1

1. If you took time to memorize and reflect on Isaiah 53:5–6, describe how this passage has deepened your understanding of God's love for you.
2. If you formed an impact list and have begun praying for the people on this list, how has this inspired you to tell others about the love of God?

THE BIG PICTURE

On a plane coming home from Dallas one day, I happened to be sitting next to a very beautiful woman. We struck up a conversation. I found out that she was dating an NBA basketball player. His was a household name . . . if I wrote it down, most of the people reading these words would recognize him.

"I bet that is exciting, isn't it?" I asked her.

"It really is," she answered. "I just spent two weeks living with this guy as we traveled with the team."

"Are you married?" I asked.

"Of course not. We are just *good* friends. We were just living with each other for the last couple of weeks. It was exciting."

She went on to say, "You ought to attend some of those parties after they win a game. They are great. We smoke a little grass. We do some coke. We party. Oh, do we party."

"You must be kind of sad, leaving that situation going back home to work," I said.

"Not really," she said, "I've got another boyfriend back home."

Then she looked at me and asked, "By the way, what do you do for a living?"

"I am a minister," I responded.

"Oh," was all she could muster.

I said, "Do you mind if I ask you sort of a technical question that those of us in the profession ask people now and then?"

"No, go ahead."

"When you participate in that kind of lifestyle, the running around, the partying, the grass, the coke, the whole shot, doesn't that make you feel a little bit guilty?"

It was like I tripped a switch. "No, it doesn't make me feel guilty," she stated adamantly. "Who do you think I am anyway? I am not an Idi Amin, Adolph Hitler type. I am a decent woman. I am well-educated, well-adjusted, I hold down a job, I am loyal to my friends. I consider myself as medium as anybody else out there."

I continued, "Well, can I ask you just one more question?" After getting her okay I said, "I am interested why you compared yourself to Idi Amin and Adolph Hitler. Why don't you compare your morality with Mother Teresa, St. Francis of Assisi, or Jesus of Nazareth?"

That about ended our conversation.

You see, this woman was doing morality by comparison. She was finding the worst examples she could think of, measuring herself against them, and patting herself on the back for how good she measured up. It would be like me saying I am a great weight lifter because I can bench press more than my grandmother. When we pick out who we want to compare ourselves to, we can come out looking pretty good.

A WIDE ANGLE VIEW

1
How do people play the comparison game in *one* of the following areas:

- Their financial status
- Their moral condition
- Their family life
- Their religious devotion

Why do we spend so much of our time drawing comparisons with the people around us?

A BIBLICAL PORTRAIT

Read Luke 16:19–31

2 In this passage, "Abraham's side" is a picture of heaven. What do you learn about heaven from this story?

What do you learn about hell?

3 Respond to *one* of these statements:

- Hell is the invention of angry and closed-minded preachers. A loving God would never send anyone to hell.
- Heaven is a state of mind. We achieve it in this life when we are kind and loving to each other.

SHARPENING THE FOCUS

Read Snapshot "How Good Is Good Enough?"

HOW GOOD IS GOOD ENOUGH?

Like the woman I met on the flight from Dallas, many people are doing morality by comparison. They hope their handful of good works, in comparison to some people who are "really bad," will make them acceptable in God's sight. What they don't realize is that the good works they are trying to add up just won't pay the price.

I remember walking onto a car lot with my son, Todd, when he was just four years old. At the time he was particularly drawn to Trans Ams. As we were walking down the row, he saw one he liked. It cost close to $20,000. Todd said, "I like this one. Let's buy it." I said, "Son, we really don't have that kind of money." He said, "I have some money!" So I asked him, "Well, how much do you have?" He responded, "I have four dimes and a nickel." I didn't quite know how to explain to him that his life savings was not even in the ballpark.

This situation is very similar to those who are counting on their morality and good works to get into heaven. When they come to stand before a holy God and find that the bill for their sin is going to be in the billions, they will rummage through their moral pockets and pull out about four dimes and a nickel. In light of God's holiness, our "good works" will never be enough.

4 Many people really think their collection of good works will be enough to get them into heaven. How would you respond to a non-Christian friend who says, "I've lived a pretty good life. I'm fairly confident I will go to heaven when I die!"

5 Why are good works never enough to get us into heaven?

If good works don't get you into heaven, why do them?

Read Snapshot "Four False Assurances"

FOUR FALSE ASSURANCES

In addition to the false assurance that good works will get them into heaven, people hold several other false assurances. Some people believe they will get into heaven because they hold to a basic set of beliefs. They say, "I believe in God. I believe Jesus lived and died." They forget that James says, "Even the demons believe that—and shudder" (James 2:19). Accepting a set of beliefs is not the same as being a Christian.

Others say they will go to heaven because they have faithfully attended church. They may have even gone to Sunday school or put a little money in the offering plate. Still others cling to the notion, that because they have been baptized, they have a sure ticket to heaven. But despite the fact that their church tradition might teach this or that they believe it with great conviction, they are wrong.

One other false assumption I have seen might ruffle a few people's spiritual feathers. Some people say, "I know I am a Christian because I raised my hand in a worship service" (or walked the aisle at a crusade, or prayed a prayer asking Jesus to come into my heart). There is more to being a Christian than one moment of public commitment. Jesus tells the parable of the sower to communicate that some people make a response but fall away because of temptations or the cares of the world. I am not saying that people who make these public responses are not Christian, but one public response does not guarantee a person has truly become a follower of Christ.

6 If you held one of these false tickets before becoming a follower of Christ, what helped you make a real and genuine commitment to be a Christian?

If you suspect you are holding one of these false assumptions about being a Christian right now, which one is it and what do you need to do to get rid of it?

7

James says, "You believe that there is one God. Good! Even the demons believe that—and shudder" (James 2:19). How is it possible to have the right set of beliefs and still not be a Christian?

What is the difference between believing things about God and believing in God?

Read Snapshot "Five Biblical Convictions"

FIVE BIBLICAL CONVICTIONS

What happens in the heart and life of a person who becomes a fully devoted follower of Christ? Though each Christian looks a little different, some common themes run through our lives. First, each Christian has come face-to-face with the truth of his own sinfulness and personal bankruptcy before God. At the same time, each comes to understand the depth of God's love for them and the forgiveness He offers only through the death of Jesus on the cross. Then each says yes to Jesus.

A second affirmation that someone is a Christian is the witness of the Holy Spirit. This is a deep inner sense that God is with you and in you. Sometimes the Spirit challenges and convicts, at other times He inspires and encourages. More and more, as time goes by, we feel the work of the Spirit within us.

Along with the subjective inner work of the Spirit comes the objective outer work of the Spirit, our third element. When you become a fully devoted follower of Christ, your behavior begins to change. You see the change and so do the people around you.

A fourth evidence of being a Christian is that a person's view of sin changes. Things that used to seem harmless and benign now stand out as offensive to God. Instead of being hard-hearted about your sin, you face the reality of guilt and remorse. Your heart breaks when you realize that your sin put Jesus on the cross.

And fifth, as this conviction grows, you discover that you have a whole new set of goals for life. Instead of seeking self-centered goals, you establish God-centered goals. Instead of saying "My will be done," you say "Thy will be done!"

8 Describe in detail your moment of truth with God.

9 Where do you see the Holy Spirit working in your life right now?

PUTTING YOURSELF IN THE PICTURE

CHANGE MY HEART

Take time in the coming week to reflect on how God is changing your view of sin. First, think back over the past one or two years. How has your view of sin changed in very specific areas?

Use the space provided to list the area of sin, your previous view of sin, and how you now view it:

Area of sin	Previous view of this sin	How you view this sin now
• _____	_____	_____
• _____	_____	_____
• _____	_____	_____

Take time to pray, thanking God for the way He is changing your view of sin.

Next, think of two or three areas of sin you are facing right now. Use the space provided to list the area, your view of this sin right now, and how you feel God wants your view to change.

Area of sin	How you view this sin	How God views this sin
• _____	_____	_____
• _____	_____	_____
• _____	_____	_____

Take time to pray for God to begin changing your view of this sin until it reflects His perspective!

MY FUTURE IS YOURS

Take time to reflect on some of the goals you have for your life right now. How do these goals reflect that you are a fully devoted follower of Christ?

My goals

- _____

- _____

- _____

- _____

What goals might God want you to set that would reflect a deep commitment to follow Him and live for Him?

- _____

- _____

- _____

- _____

KEYS TO SPIRITUAL GROWTH

REFLECTIONS FROM SESSION 2

1. If you took time since your last small group to evaluate your view of sin, describe one area in which your view of sin has changed.
2. What is one goal you have in becoming a more fully devoted follower of Christ?

THE BIG PICTURE

Some years ago I read a book by Charles Colson entitled *Loving God*. It was a time when I was deeply seeking to grow as a follower of Christ and was trying to discern God's leading in my life. I had the sense that if I spent a little extra time reading Colson's book that God had something in it for me. That is exactly what happened. The book was what I needed to hear from God. It was insightful, convicting, hard-hitting, challenging, and inspirational. As I read the last few words and put the book down, I nearly wept as I thanked God for how He had met a specific need in my life through the writing of Charles Colson. God was helping me grow through another follower of Christ.

At the same time, another thought exploded in my mind. I remembered, years earlier, being a youth leader at a camp with a hundred junior high boys. I recall one leader from the church couldn't come right away but came later in the week. When he got out of his car he had a rather sober look on his face. He said, "You won't believe what just happened. President Nixon resigned." As the drama unfolded and the details came out, the nation discovered that Chuck Colson was, by his own admission, a corrupt, power-intoxicated, hard-hearted nonbeliever. He too was involved in the Watergate scandal.

Over time, Chuck Colson recognized his sin, admitted his need for a personal Savior, and trusted Christ to be his forgiver and the leader of his life. It soon became clear to many people that Chuck Colson was a changed man. Slowly, steadily, month by month, year by year, lesson by lesson, truth by truth, he was transformed. Now here I was reading a book he had written to feed pastors, challenge seminary professors, and bring new lessons to bear on churches. This was a man who had experienced radical Christian growth.

A WIDE ANGLE VIEW

1 How have you been growing as a follower of Christ over the past year?

Who is one follower of Christ that you look to as an example? What do you learn from this person?

A BIBLICAL PORTRAIT

Read Acts 2:38–47

2 What actions marked the lives of the early Christians?

Where do you see these same actions among Christ followers today?

Which of these actions are missing in the lives of many Christians today?

3 What attitudes marked the lives of the early Christians?

Where do you see these same attitudes among Christ followers today?

Which of these attitudes are missing in the lives of many Christians today?

SHARPENING THE FOCUS

Read Snapshot "Devoted to Learning"

DEVOTED TO LEARNING

The first key to Christian growth is to devote ourselves to God's teaching. The members of the early church realized that one of the primary ways God has ordained for Christians to grow is to sit under the teaching of pastors. A commitment to growth through personal reading of the Bible is critical, but the Bible also teaches that something supernatural happens when all of the believers assemble together. Lives change. People grow.

Sometimes I get letters from people who write to tell me that God spoke to them through a message I preached. When they thank me for this I always have to write them back and say, "Please understand, this is the miracle of Christian growth. When we all gather together and study the Bible, something supernatural happens." Sometimes as I preach God's Word I can feel that broken hearts are being mended by the Holy Spirit, rebellious hearts are being softened, proud hearts are being humbled, and cold hearts are being warmed up.

4 Describe a time when God spoke clearly and directly to you through the preaching/teaching of His Word.

5 In the course of a week, where do you hear God's Word preached/taught?

How can your group members encourage you to be more faithful and consistent in the discipline of hearing God's Word preached/taught?

Read Snapshot "Committed to Fellowship"

COMMITTED TO FELLOWSHIP

The early Christians also devoted themselves to fellowship. That doesn't simply mean that every once in awhile they had lunch with a fellow believer, nor does it mean they had a short conversation with someone in the lobby after the service. It means they devoted themselves to one another in deep, significant, transparent relationships.

We are not a collection of Lone Rangers. God created us to be in community with one another, and we grow best when we interface our growth with brothers and sisters in Christ. When we receive good teaching it is essential to interact, question, discuss, and challenge what we have heard. This happens best in community. We also need to hold one another accountable for fleshing out what we have learned. A commitment to fellowship with other followers of Christ is essential for our growth.

---

6 If you are deeply committed to fellowship and connected with other Christians, how is this helping you grow in your faith?

If you are lacking in this area, what can you do to deepen ties of fellowship with other followers of Christ in the coming days?

Read Snapshot "A Hunger for Communion"

A HUNGER FOR COMMUNION

It was a few days before Christmas and we had just moved into a new home. We had a lot of things still in boxes but Lynne had dug out some pictures and put them in my study. I picked up a picture of my dad and myself standing in front of his airplane. It was taken about two weeks before he died. Instantly, it was like a floodgate of emotion opening. The full memory of who my dad was and how significant he was in my life came cascading down on me. I sat down on the couch and had a quiet and sacred moment of reminiscing. That picture became a tangible reminder of someone very important to me.

This is the very reason God has given us communion. Before Jesus died, He told His followers to celebrate communion often and remember Him. Jesus knew we would get caught up in service, relationships, Bible study, work, raising kids, and lots of other good and important things. However, He wanted to be sure we would take time on a regular basis to remember Him! He knew we would grow best if we kept our focus on Him. This is why we take the bread and the cup; they remind us of the One who loves us beyond description. These moments open the floodgates and help us reminisce about what Jesus means to us.

7

How does celebrating communion help you focus on Jesus and remind you of His love for you?

How does this experience spur you on to Christian growth?

Read Snapshot "A Passion for Prayer"

A PASSION FOR PRAYER

The New Testament tells us that the early Christians devoted themselves to prayer. When we read about the early church we discover prayer was in the center of their personal lives and in the heart of their life as a community.

Prayer is a God-ordained privilege of communication with our heavenly Father. He calls us, invites us, to communicate with Him. When praying, remember to keep your prayers conversational. God is not impressed by lingo, vain repetition, or empty words. Learn to talk to God like you talk to a friend. Also, prayers should be transparent. Psalm 62:8 tells us to pour our hearts before Him. Honesty in our prayers is absolutely essential!

8

What helps you communicate openly with God?

What stands in the way of your communicating openly with God in prayer?

9

What do you need your small group members to pray for in *one* of these areas:

- In your spiritual growth
- In your family life
- In your professional life
- In a friendship

Express one joy or praise you want to invite your small group members to celebrate in prayer with you.

PUTTING YOURSELF IN THE PICTURE

POURING YOUR HEART OUT TO GOD

The psalmist invites us to deep honesty and transparency in our prayers. Take time in the coming week to memorize this portion of Psalm 62. Pray for a heart that will be completely open to God in prayer.

> *Find rest, O my soul, in God alone;*
> *my hope comes from him.*
> *He alone is my rock and my salvation;*
> *he is my fortress, I will not be shaken.*
> *My salvation and my honor depend on God;*
> *he is my mighty rock, my refuge.*
> *Trust in him at all times, O people;*
> *pour out your hearts to him,*
> *for God is our refuge.*
>
> PSALM 62:5–8

GROWTH METER

Take an honest look at each of the growth areas studied in this session. On a scale of 1 to 10, how are you doing in making forward progression toward growth in each area? What can you do to increase growth in the weaker areas? What can you do to continue growing in your areas of strength? How can your group members encourage you and keep you accountable for growth in your Christian life?

Growth Through Biblical Teaching

1	2	3	4	5	6	7	8	9	10
No growth		*Little growth*		*Some growth*		*Steady growth*		*Rapid growth*	

35

Growth Through Fellowship

1	2	3	4	5	6	7	8	9	10
No growth		Little growth		Some growth		Steady growth		Rapid growth	

Growth Through Communion

1	2	3	4	5	6	7	8	9	10
No growth		Little growth		Some growth		Steady growth		Rapid growth	

Growth Through Prayer

1	2	3	4	5	6	7	8	9	10
No growth		Little growth		Some growth		Steady growth		Rapid growth	

Getting Up After Falling Down

Reflections from Session 3

1. If you memorized and reflected on Psalm 62:5–8, how has this passage deepened your prayer life?
2. If you did the "Growth Meter" exercise, where did you see encouraging spiritual growth in your life? What was one area in which you sense a need for focused spiritual growth?

THE BIG PICTURE

Do you know what three-letter word is one of the most important words in the vocabulary of a fully devoted follower of Christ? What three-letter word is all-important as we seek to grow in our understanding of who God is and in our relationship with God through Jesus Christ? The word is "yes."

If you think about it, nothing of any consequence will ever happen to someone spiritually until he or she begins to say yes to God. When we first begin to seek God, it is essential to be open to His Word. In reading and hearing God's Word, we discover that every single person has fallen short of God's standard of moral perfection. In biblical terms, every person is a sinner. When we hear or read this for the first time, there comes a moment of truth. What do we say to God when He says that every single person (including us) has fallen short of His standard? If we are going to get anywhere spiritually, there is only one right answer: "Yes."

Along the way we discover, through God's Word, that not only have we sinned, but because of our sin, we need a Savior. We need someone who can forgive, cleanse, and transform us from the inside out. What response is essential for us to take the next step toward God, to experience that cleansing? It is just one word: "Yes!"

Jesus Christ is the only person who can offer forgiveness. Acts 4:12 teaches us there is salvation in no other name. We need to agree with God about our condition and say, "Yes, I am a sinner. I am in desperate need of a Savior. His name is Jesus Christ. My response to Him now and forever is 'yes.'"

When we say yes to God, we quickly discover there is another power vying for authority in our life. Every time we come to a moment of truth, the Holy Spirit of God says to us, "Say yes," while the forces of hell cry out, "Say no!" Satan urges, "Hey Christian, don't you get tired of always doing things God's way? You pushover. You don't even use your mind, you just do what God says. Why not start doing things your way?"

Can you identify with this battle? Satan continues to repeat a pack of lies that are as old as history itself. "What are you hesitating for?" he says. "Saying no to God isn't a big deal. He won't do anything. You are only human. There won't be any consequences. There are lots of people saying no to God and they still have nice houses, good jobs, and happy lives. Besides, obedience is a drag." On and on the enemy lies until our minds begin to spin out of control and we find ourselves saying the two-letter word that plunged society into darkness.

A WIDE ANGLE VIEW

1 Describe a time you said yes to God. What fruit came from this act of obedience?

Tell about a time you said no to God. What were some of the consequences?

A BIBLICAL PORTRAIT

Read Psalm 1

2 What characteristics mark the life of a person who says yes to God (v.1–3)?

What will this kind of life produce?

3 What characteristics mark the life of a person who consistently says no to God (v.4–6)?

What will this kind of life produce?

SHARPENING THE FOCUS

Read Snapshot "Never Say No to God"

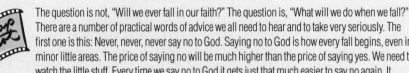

NEVER SAY NO TO GOD

The question is not, "Will we ever fall in our faith?" The question is, "What will we do when we fall?" There are a number of practical words of advice we all need to hear and to take very seriously. The first one is this: Never, never, never say no to God. Saying no to God is how every fall begins, even in minor little areas. The price of saying no will be much higher than the price of saying yes. We need to watch the little stuff. Every time we say no to God it gets just that much easier to say no again. It doesn't take long before saying no becomes a pattern in our lives. We must make a decision to do everything it takes to resist saying no to God.

4 Describe a specific situation in your life right now in which you are being tempted to say no to God.

How can your group members pray for you and keep you accountable to say yes to God in this area?

Read Snapshot "Say Yes to God's Word"

SAY YES TO GOD'S WORD

A second practical word of advice to those who want to be fully devoted followers of Christ is to say yes to God as often as possible. When you read God's Word and receive practical direction for your life, follow it! When God's Word calls you to change an attitude or behavior in your life, change it. When the Holy Spirit prompts you to connect with a specific person or drop someone an encouraging note, do it as soon as possible. Commit yourself to say yes to God every chance you get. You will quickly discover that saying yes to God will help you develop a lifestyle of obedience in every area.

---

5 Tell your group about an area in your life in which you have been sensing God's leading but in which you have still not said yes.

What will it take to give you that final push and move you to say yes to God in this area?

6 Describe an area in your life in which you have been learning to say yes to God. How has it grown easier to say yes over time?

Read Snapshot "Take Your Sins to Jesus"

TAKE YOUR SINS TO JESUS

We all need to avoid saying no to God and learn to begin saying yes. However, when we fall—and we all fall—we need to take that sin to the Lord Jesus Christ before the sun sets. The enemy will want to bury us in guilt, cripple us with fear, and keep us from going to the only One who can give us forgiveness. When we fall into sin, we have hit an ASAP moment. We need to get face-to-face with our Savior, confess our sins, commit ourselves to change, and accept His cleansing.

7 How have you experienced God's forgiveness and love when you have come to Him and confessed your sins?

Read Snapshot "Confess Your Sins to Each Other"

CONFESS YOUR SINS TO EACH OTHER

James 5:16 says, "Therefore confess your sins to each other and pray for each other so that you may be healed . . ." One more important part in the process of getting up after we fall is learning the wisdom and power of confession. Not only do we confess our sins to God, but we are called to confess our sins to each other and to invite others to uphold us in prayer.

It looks something like this. After we have fallen in an area of sin, we go to a brother or sister we trust, sit down with them and say, "You have to know something about me. I fell. I said no to God. It was my own fault. I am not blaming it on anyone but myself. I have confessed it to God and am committing myself to say yes to God in this area, but I want you to know so that you can pray for me and keep me accountable to obey God." This confession may sound scary, but it is an essential part of our community life together.

8 Why are we so reluctant to confess our sins to each other?

What warning would you give each other as you begin a habit of confessing your sins to each other?

9 Many sins should be confessed in a one-on-one context. Others can be confessed to more than one person. If you feel led to confess a sin to your group members, how can your group members pray for you in this area of your life?

PUTTING YOURSELF IN THE PICTURE

PLANT THESE VERSES DEEPLY

When I lead a small group, I insist that the people in the group memorize four forgiveness verses. These verses help us to silence the accusations from Satan. Take time to read and memorize these passages. Let them fill your mind and heart.

"No longer will a man teach his neighbor, or a man his brother, saying, 'Know the LORD,' because they will all know me, from the least of them to the greatest," declares the LORD. For I will forgive their wickedness and will remember their sins no more.

JEREMIAH 31:34

"Come now, let us reason together," says the LORD. "Though your sins are like scarlet, they shall be as white as snow; though they are red as crimson, they shall be like wool.

ISAIAH 1:18

As far as the east is from the west, so far has he removed our transgressions from us.

PSALM 103:12

In him we have redemption through his blood, the forgiveness of sins, in accordance with the riches of God's grace.

EPHESIANS 1:7

THE POWER OF CONFESSION

Take time to identify one or two areas in which you are saying no to God. Confess your sin in these areas to God and commit yourself to begin saying yes to Him. Also, identify one other follower of Christ you trust deeply and commit yourself to confess this sin to them. Ask this person to pray for you and keep you accountable to say yes to God in this area of your life.

BEING CHRISTIAN IN A NON-CHRISTIAN WORLD

REFLECTIONS FROM SESSION 4

1. If you memorized the four verses on forgiveness, how has planting these portions of Scripture in your heart impacted your view of how God sees you?
2. If you have committed yourself to openly confess your sins to God and other followers of Christ, how has this commitment helped you grow in your faith?

THE BIG PICTURE

Harry, like so many people, thought that he was born a Christian. Some months ago, however, he came to grips with the fact that the Bible says we are all born in sin—no one is born a Christian. We then validate this truth by making sinful choices.

Harry looked at his life and at the claims of the Christian faith as he considered what was required to become a Christian. After some time of seeking and searching, he called on Jesus Christ to become his forgiver and the leader of his life. He confessed his sin. There was no voice from heaven. The clouds didn't part. There was, however, a type of calm that only a follower of Christ can truly understand. Harry had become a Christian.

In the next few days and weeks the Holy Spirit began to help Harry understand a little more of what this decision actually meant. As time went on, Harry not only experienced the peace of the Holy Spirit, but he also began to feel an assurance and confidence. A new joy filled his heart. A love for God and sensitivity for people began to blossom in his life. Later, a sense of purpose and destiny began to emerge. Harry began to dream big dreams about doing something with his life.

Harry began living with a profound understanding that his eternity was secure and that heaven awaited him. He had a growing sense of well-being and security. He found his heart nearly bursting with praise, wonder, and appreciation. The good news of all God had done for him, the joy of all God was doing, and the hope of all God promised for the future was almost too much for Harry to take! There was no way he could keep it to himself.

Harry began to feel a genuine desire, from deep within, to tell others about Jesus. Most of all he wanted to tell his friend Frank about the change in his life. *I've found what Frank is looking for!* Harry thought. *I've got what he needs. I have to talk to him about it right away. Tomorrow at lunch I'll tell Frank all about Jesus!* That night Harry planned, prepared, and prayed. The next day he went to work saying, "This is Frank's lucky day. His life will be changed like mine!" Harry was excited and filled with anticipation. At lunch, Harry sat Frank down and told him the whole story.

A WIDE ANGLE VIEW

1 Finish the story above. What is one way Harry's lunch with Frank could have ended?

Describe a time you told someone about your faith in Christ and how that person responded.

A BIBLICAL PORTRAIT

Read Matthew 5:13–16

2 What qualities of light should a Christ follower seek to emulate?

What qualities of salt should a Christ follower seek to emulate?

3 What does it mean to let your light shine?

SHARPENING THE FOCUS

Read Snapshot "Secret Ambassadors"

SECRET AMBASSADORS

Every follower of Christ is called to be an ambassador. There are many different types of ambassadors. One kind is what I call a secret ambassador. This is a follower of Christ who functions much like a double agent, changing like a chameleon with each situation. The potency of their salt is weak and their light is very dim, if it is shining at all. These people work hard at keeping their Christian faith in the closet.

I remember meeting a Hollywood producer at a gathering of Christian leaders from all over the country. When he listed all the movies he had worked on, we realized he was a person of real influence in the Hollywood scene. Before the gathering was over, he asked some of us to keep from mentioning that he was at a gathering of evangelical Christian leaders. He was afraid this information could hurt his opportunities on some "really exciting projects" in his future. He was doing all he could to keep his faith hidden. This man was a secret ambassador.

4 Create a profile of a secret ambassador. What does a secret ambassador look like?

Do you see any of these characteristics in your life?

5 Identify some of the consequences of living as a secret ambassador in *one* of these areas:

- Our growth as followers of Christ
- Our opportunities to tell others about Jesus
- Our view of ourselves as Christians
- How other Christians view us
- How seekers view us

Read Snapshot "Obnoxious Ambassadors"

OBNOXIOUS AMBASSADORS

In dramatic contrast to the secret ambassador is the obnoxious ambassador. This is the type of person who throws good judgment, common sense, and diplomacy out the window. An obnoxious ambassador equates boldness, aggressiveness, and an "in-your-face" approach with godliness.

The problem is that this kind of ambassador ends up doing more harm than good. An obnoxious ambassador barges in uninvited, shouts answers when no one is asking questions, offers two-cent slogans for million-dollar mysteries, preaches, pushes, and presses until unbelievers are no longer rejecting the message of Christ as much as they are rejecting this overbearing messenger.

We have to be careful that we don't get so bold and aggressive that we become obnoxious and violate those very people we want to reach. We want our light to shine, but putting a spotlight directly in people's eyes only blinds them! Almost every person I know has been offended, at one time or another, by an overzealous Christian. Because of this, we need to make a conscious decision not to be obnoxious ambassadors.

6 Describe a time you were confronted by an obnoxious ambassador. What impact did this have on you?

7

What is the balance between an obnoxious ambassador and a secret ambassador?

How are you seeking to strike this balance in your life?

Read Snapshot "Spirit-Led Ambassadors"

SPIRIT-LED AMBASSADORS

Secret ambassadors blend in with their surroundings. No one would ever know they are Christ followers. Obnoxious ambassadors stand out like a sore thumb. They let everyone know they are Christians, too often communicating things in a way that puts people off rather than drawing them closer to Christ. In contrast to both of these types of ambassadors is a Spirit-led ambassador.

Spirit-led ambassadors have discovered that there are no formulas for communicating their faith. Instead, they seek the leading of God's Spirit in every situation they encounter. Some situations call for a gentle, quiet approach in helping someone learn about Christ. In other cases, the Spirit leads them to confronting someone with a bold, direct approach. Every person and situation demands a new way of communicating about Christ.

Imagine a follower of Christ sitting with a group of people when someone uses God's name in vain. The secret ambassador does nothing—there is no need to make waves or offend anyone. The obnoxious ambassador cries out, "Let no unwholesome word proceed out of our mouth. Thou shall not take the name of the Lord thy God in vain!" polarizing everyone and burning relational bridges. But the Spirit-led ambassador begins to pray silently, *O God, what shall I do at this moment? Should I gently confront this person in love or wait for another time? What is the best way to communicate to this person?* The Spirit-led ambassador does not have some automatic knee-jerk reaction but relies on the Holy Spirit for wisdom in all of life's situations.

8 Choose *one* of these scenarios and identify how you feel each of the three different ambassadors (secret, obnoxious, and Spirit-led) would respond:

- A follower of Christ is on an airplane sitting next to an attractive woman. "So, what do you do for a living?" the Christian asks. The woman responds, "I am an exotic dancer."
- A follower of Christ moves into a new home and discovers that his next door neighbor is a Muslim.
- A follower of Christ is invited to go out for drinks after work with some fellow employees.

9 Who is one person in your life right now toward whom you are trying to be a Spirit-led ambassador?

What is the Spirit leading you to say and do in this relationship that would help this person come to know Christ?

PUTTING YOURSELF IN THE PICTURE

You Are the Light of the World

Because you are the light of the world, take time to memorize Matthew 5:14. Reflect on the implications of this passage and pray for a deeper understanding of yourself as one who shines God's light in every life situation.

> You are the light of the world. A city on a hill cannot be hidden.

Ambassador Assessment

Reflect honestly on your life and determine what kind of ambassador you are in a variety of situations. You might be surprised to discover that you are a Spirit-led ambassador in some areas and a secret ambassador or obnoxious ambassador in other areas. Pray through each area and ask God to teach you to be a Spirit-led ambassador in every area.

- Among my extended family members I am functioning as a (circle one):

Secret ambassador	Obnoxious ambassador	Spirit-led ambassador

- In my workplace I am functioning as a (circle one):

Secret ambassador	Obnoxious ambassador	Spirit-led ambassador

- In my neighborhood I am functioning as a (circle one):

Secret ambassador	Obnoxious ambassador	Spirit-led ambassador

- In my social settings I am functioning as a (circle one):

Secret ambassador	Obnoxious ambassador	Spirit-led ambassador

- In my friendships with seekers I am functioning as a (circle one):

Secret ambassador	Obnoxious ambassador	Spirit-led ambassador

Take time to pray through each area and ask God to teach you how to be stronger salt and brighter light. Pray that you would become an effective Spirit-led ambassador in every area of your life.

GUIDANCE ALONG THE WAY

REFLECTIONS FROM SESSION 5

1. If you have been reflecting on what it means to be the "light of the world," how have you been light in a dark place since our last session?
2. If you took the ambassador assessment, what was one area in which you sense God is using you as a Spirit-led ambassador? What was one area of life you discovered in which you need to develop as God's ambassador?

THE BIG PICTURE

One of the most frightening and frustrating experiences in life is being lost. We can all remember times when we have been lost and the flood of emotions that comes with this experience. Have you ever been hiking in the woods and realized that you have lost your way and that the sun will be setting soon? Or a time when you were driving on an unfamiliar freeway and discovered that whoever was in charge of handling the directions was not doing a great job? Or being lost in an airport and knowing your plane was leaving at any moment? Most of us can remember back to a time in our childhood when we became separated from our parents and the fear this brought until we were finally found.

I know the feeling of being lost all too well. When I was taking pilot's lessons for flying private airplanes, my first solo cross-country flight turned out to be more memorable than I would have wanted. In making a cross-country flight of several hundred miles, I miscalculated the wind drift angle and ended up way off course. I got so lost that I had to fly down and read the names of the cities on the water towers. I circled a water tower and read the name of the city, then looked for the city on my map. When I located it I thought, "This can't be!" I flew back down and read it again. I could not believe how far off course I had flown.

Another time I was flying in bad weather and couldn't venture beneath the clouds. I had not received a rating that allowed me to fly by instruments, so I had to radio in for radar vectors. "Excuse me. I have no idea where I am. Could you just tell me where to point my plane?" It was a rather humbling experience, to say the least. I can still recall how thankful I was to hear a calm reassuring voice on the other end of the radio giving me directions with pinpoint accuracy to help guide me through the storm and lead me safely to the ground.

A WIDE ANGLE VIEW

1 Describe a time you were lost. How old were you, where were you, how did you feel?

How did you "get found" or find your way out of this situation?

A BIBLICAL PORTRAIT

Read Psalm 23

2 Psalm 23 is often used at funerals or read near the time of death. Though this is an appropriate time to reflect on this psalm, it also has a powerful message for the living. It gives profound insight and encouragement for how God wants to give us guidance in our lives. According to this psalm, how does God guide His people?

What parallels do you see between a shepherd leading His sheep and God leading His followers?

3 What do you learn about the heart of God toward His followers in this psalm?

SHARPENING THE FOCUS

Read Snapshot "Guidance from the Bible"

GUIDANCE FROM THE BIBLE

The primary way God guides His children is through his Word, the Bible. The minute some people hear the word "Bible" they begin thinking BORING! They say, "I don't want a Bible study. I want a vision in 3–D technicolor, with surround sound. I want an angel to speak to me personally. I want a leaflet from heaven. I want a divine road map. I want the clouds to part." The idea of studying the Bible seems so mundane and ordinary. However, for those followers of Christ who really want to know God's leading in their life, the Bible is essential. Psalm 119:105 says, "Your word is a lamp to my feet and a light for my path."

One Christian leader named Paul Little was quoted as saying, "Ninety percent of God's will for your life has already been revealed in His Word." At first glance this may seem like an overstatement. But, when you stop to think about it, the Bible gives specific instructions in so many areas of life. God's Word teaches us about what our character and conduct should look like. It gives direction for making wise career choices, choosing a spouse, loving that spouse, raising children, handling personal finances, growing spiritually, caring for our body, making our life count for Christ, and so much more. Sometimes I wish I could say I'm lost in the fog. The truth is, it is not what I do not know about the pathway for my life that bothers me as much as what I *do* know about the type of person I am supposed to be becoming. I do believe that ninety percent of God's will for our lives is already spelled out in His Word.

Respond to *one* of these statements:

- I have read the Bible before, and it seemed dry and boring.
- The Bible was written thousands of years ago; it doesn't speak to modern-day issues!

5

Fully devoted followers of Christ need to be committed to knowing the Bible. We need the Spirit-led, creative, vital experience of reading the Bible on a regular basis. However, reading the Bible should not be about a legalistic and rigid pattern of daily study. What personal habits or disciplines have you established so that you are growing in God's Word?

What habits do you need to develop?

How can your group members encourage you and keep you accountable to be a man or woman of the Word?

Read Snapshot "The Inner Guidance of the Holy Spirit"

THE INNER GUIDANCE OF THE HOLY SPIRIT

 The Bible answers many of life's questions. However, there are many questions that are not answered directly in Scripture. Should I go to college or start a career? Should I change careers and begin looking for a new job? Should I marry this particular person? How do I select the right church? Should we start a family at this time? The list of questions goes on and on. What do you do when you are looking for more specific guidance?

God has graciously afforded us direction through the inner witness of the Holy Spirit. When you become a Christian, God places His Holy Spirit in your life. One of the roles of the Spirit is guidance. The Spirit tends to begin guiding by bringing an unrest within us—a sense of prompting, a feeling of being unsettled. This will often move us to prayer. We begin seeking God's direction in a specific area of life. At this point, God will often call us aside for times of silence, solitude, and listening. In these private moments with God we begin to feel a leading or direction and, with a humble heart before Him, we begin moving in the direction we sense He is prompting. Along the way, He will confirm we are in His will by bringing peace in our heart, affirmation in our spirit, and wisdom from other Christian brothers and sisters. When we are heading in the wrong direction, the Spirit will bring unrest and a lack of peace. God can also close doors or send other Christ followers to redirect us. The key is to move where you sense the Spirit is leading, yet to remain humble and open for new direction along the way.

---

6 Tell about a time you sensed the Spirit's leading, followed it, and found yourself right in the middle of God's will.

How did the Spirit lead and prompt you in this process?

7

What is one area in your life in which you need the
Spirit's leading right now?

*How can your small group pray for you as you seek God's
leading in this area of your life?*

Read Snapshot "Guidance Through Other Christ Followers"

GUIDANCE THROUGH OTHER CHRIST FOLLOWERS

God also lovingly affords us counsel through His people. There is great wisdom in seeking insight and counsel from other followers of Christ. Presidents often have counselors, businessmen hire consultants, and coaches have assistants, yet in the church we have far too many people who are too proud and independent to admit their need for input and instruction from godly brothers and sisters.

The truth is, we can all be biased, self-willed, and easily self-deceived. We can fail to make the right decisions. Sometimes we are too close to things to exercise the wisdom we need. However, God can use mature believers to speak His words of guidance to us. All around us are godly, seasoned, experienced followers of Christ. We need to learn to pour out our heart to them and allow God to speak through their words and life. Godly brothers and sisters can check our thinking, give us feedback, and help us see if our decisions are aligned with Scripture. With the counsel of others, we get clearer direction from God, make fewer mistakes, and learn to develop closer bonds of community with other Christians.

8 Who is one fully devoted follower of Christ in your life to whom you look for wisdom and guidance? How has God used this person in your life?

9 Not only does God use individuals to give us guidance, but He can use groups of people who are fully devoted Christ followers. How can your small group become a place where mutual counsel and wisdom is communicated?

PUTTING YOURSELF IN THE PICTURE

CLEARING THE WAY FOR GUIDANCE

Some people might have to honestly say, "I have never received guidance in my whole Christian life. I have always wanted to sense God's leading, but it just never seemed to come." Do you know what can cut off God's guidance quicker than anything else? The answer is sin. When we have a pattern of disobedience in our life or a streak of rebellion in our heart, the door to God's guidance begins to close.

We also cut off the guidance process through our self-will. There is a big difference between humbly saying, "God, I will submit to Your guidance" and pridefully saying, "God, I'd like You to put Your stamp of approval on my plans." Our self-will can stand in the way of our sensing God's guidance in our lives.

One other item that stands in the way of us receiving guidance from God is impatience. It is difficult to wait on the Lord, to wrestle, to submit, to pray, to walk, to plead, to trust, but the process is as precious as the end product. Nothing produces Christian character like being in the process of searching for guidance from God.

Take time in the coming weeks to search your heart and life and see if any of these roadblocks are standing in the way of God granting you His guidance. Where you discover sin, confess it. Where you see self-will, surrender it. Where there is impatience, pray for the fruit of patience to grow and blossom in your life. Ask God to remove these obstacles so you can experience His guidance fully.

An Exercise in Listening

Take twenty to thirty minutes some time in the coming week to seek the Holy Spirit's guidance through listening. Choose a place and time where you can be alone. Bring only a blank sheet of paper and a pencil. Ask the following questions, one at a time, and wait in silence for the Holy Spirit to speak quietly to your heart. Write down just a few words to remind you of the prompting you sensed from the Spirit.

- Is there any action or behavior in my life You want me to stop?
- Is there any action or behavior You want me to begin?
- Is there a person I have wronged? If so, how should I approach that person to ask for forgiveness?
- Is there a person who has wronged me whom I have not yet forgiven?
- Is there a person You want me to care for, to serve, or to show love? What would You have me do?
- Is there any sin in my life that I need to confess and change my actions?

If you take time to ask these questions and listen for the voice of God through the Holy Spirit, you will begin the process of seeking this kind of spiritual guidance. As you look at these questions, you might begin to realize why many people don't seek this kind of guidance—many of us don't really want to hear God speak to us in these areas. You see, when He speaks, He expects us to respond. This can bring fear, but it also leads us into a life like no other. To hear the voice of God, to follow Him, to go where He leads, to be a fully devoted follower of Christ, is what life is all about!

LEADER'S NOTES

Leading a Bible discussion—especially for the first time—can make you feel both nervous and excited. If you are nervous, realize that you are in good company. Many biblical leaders, such as Moses, Joshua, and the apostle Paul, felt nervous and inadequate to lead others (see, for example, 1 Cor. 2:3). Yet God's grace was sufficient for them, just as it will be for you.

Some excitement is also natural. Your leadership is a gift to the others in the group. Keep in mind, however, that other group members also share responsibility for the group. Your role is simply to stimulate discussion by asking questions and encouraging people to respond. The suggestions listed below can help you to be an effective leader.

PREPARING TO LEAD

1. Ask God to help you understand and apply the passage to your own life. Unless that happens, you will not be prepared to lead others.
2. Carefully work through each question in the study guide. Meditate and reflect on the passage as you formulate your answers.
3. Familiarize yourself with the Leader's Notes for each session. These will help you understand the purpose of the session and will provide valuable information about the questions in the session. The Leader's Notes are not intended to be read to the group. These notes are primarily for your use as a group leader and for your preparation. However, when you find a section that relates well to your group, you may want to read a brief portion or encourage them to read this section at another time.
4. Pray for the various members of the group. Ask God to use these sessions to make you better disciples of Jesus Christ.
5. Before the first session, make sure each person has a study guide. Encourage them to prepare beforehand for each session.

LEADING THE SESSION

1. Begin the session on time. If people realize that the session begins on schedule, they will work harder to arrive on time.

2. At the beginning of your first time together, explain that these sessions are designed to be discussions, not lectures. Encourage everyone to participate, but realize some may be hesitant to speak during the first few sessions.

3. Don't be afraid of silence. People in the group may need time to think before responding.

4. Avoid answering your own questions. If necessary, rephrase a question until it is clearly understood. Even an eager group will quickly become passive and silent if they think the leader will do most of the talking.

5. Encourage more than one answer to each question. Ask, "What do the rest of you think?" or "Anyone else?" until several people have had a chance to respond.

6. Try to be affirming whenever possible. Let people know you appreciate their insights into the passage.

7. Never reject an answer. If it is clearly wrong, ask, "Which verse led you to that conclusion?" Or let the group handle the problem by asking them what they think about the question.

8. Avoid going off on tangents. If people wander off course, gently bring them back to the passage being considered.

9. Conclude your time together with conversational prayer. Ask God to help you apply those things that you learned in the session.

10. End on time. This will be easier if you control the pace of the discussion by not spending too much time on some questions or too little on others.

We encourage all small group leaders to use *Leading Life-Changing Small Groups* (Zondervan) by Bill Donahue and the Willow Creek Small Group Team while leading their group. Developed and used by Willow Creek Community Church, this guide is an excellent resource for training and equipping followers of Christ to effectively lead small groups. It includes valuable information on how to utilize fun and creative relationship-building exercises for your group; how to plan your meeting; how to share the leadership load by identifying, developing, and working with an "apprentice leader"; and how to find creative ways to do group prayer. In addition, the book includes material and tips on handling potential conflicts and difficult personalities, forming group covenants, inviting new members, improving listening skills, studying the Bible, and much more. Using *Leading Life-Changing Small Groups* will help you create a group that members love to be a part of.

Now let's discuss the different elements of this small group study guide and how to use them for the session portion of your group meeting.

THE BIG PICTURE

Each session will begin with a short story or overview of the lesson theme. This is called "The Big Picture" because it introduces the central theme of the session. You will need to read this section as a group or have group members read it on their own before discussion begins. Here are three ways you can approach this section of the small group session:

- As the group leader, read this section out loud for the whole group and then move into the questions in the next section, "A Wide Angle View." (You might read the first week, but then use the other two options below to encourage group involvement.)
- Ask a group member to volunteer to read this section for the group. This allows another group member to participate. It is best to ask someone in advance to give them time to read over the section before reading it to the group. It is also good to ask someone to volunteer, and not to assign this task. Some people do not feel comfortable reading in front of a group. After a group member has read this section out loud, move into the discussion questions.
- Allow time at the beginning of the session for each person to read this section silently. If you do this, be sure to allow enough time for everyone to finish reading so they can think about what they've read and be ready for meaningful discussion.

A WIDE ANGLE VIEW

This section includes one or more questions that move the group into a general discussion of the session topic. These questions are designed to help group members begin discussing the topic in an open and honest manner. Once the topic of the lesson has been established, move on to the Bible passage for the session.

A BIBLICAL PORTRAIT

This portion of the session includes a Scripture reading and one or more questions that help group members see how the theme of the session is rooted and based in biblical teaching. The Scripture reading can be handled just like "The Big Picture" section: You can read it for the group, have a group member read it, or allow time for silent reading. Make sure everyone has a Bible or that you have Bibles available for those who need them. Once you have read the passage, ask the question(s) in this section so that group members can dig into the truth of the Bible.

SHARPENING THE FOCUS

The majority of the discussion questions for the session are in this section. These questions are practical and help group members apply biblical teaching to their daily lives.

SNAPSHOTS

The "Snapshots" in each session help prepare group members for discussion. These anecdotes give additional insight to the topic being discussed. Each "Snapshot" should be read at a designated point in the session. This is clearly marked in the session as well as in the Leader's Notes. Again, follow the same format as you do with "The Big Picture" section and the "Biblical Portrait" section: Either you read the anecdote, have a group member volunteer to read, or provide time for silent reading. However you approach this section, you will find these anecdotes very helpful in triggering lively dialogue and moving discussion in a meaningful direction.

PUTTING YOURSELF IN THE PICTURE

Here's where you roll up your sleeves and put the truth into action. This portion is very practical and action-oriented. At the end of each session there will be suggestions for one or two ways group members can put what they've just learned into practice. Review the action goals at the end of each session and challenge group members to work on one or more of them in the coming week.

You will find follow-up questions for the "Putting Yourself in the Picture" section at the beginning of the next week's session. Starting with the second week, there will be time set aside at the beginning of the session to look back and talk about how you have tried to apply God's Word in your life since your last time together.

PRAYER

You will want to open and close your small group with a time of prayer. Occasionally, there will be specific direction within a session for how you can do this. Most of the time, however, you will need to decide the best place to stop and pray. You may want to pray or have a group member volunteer to begin the lesson with a prayer. Or you might want to read "The Big Picture" and discuss the "Wide Angle View" questions before opening in prayer. In some cases, it might be best to open in prayer after you have read the Bible passage. You need to decide where you feel an opening prayer best fits for your group.

When opening in prayer, think in terms of the session theme and pray for group members (including yourself) to be responsive to the truth of Scripture and the working of the Holy Spirit. If you have seekers in your group (people investigating Christianity but not yet believers) be sensitive to your expectations for group prayer. Seekers may not yet be ready to take part in group prayer.

Be sure to close your group with a time of prayer as well. One option is for you to pray for the entire group. Or you might allow time for group members to offer audible prayers that others can agree with in their hearts. Another approach would be to allow a time of silence for one-on-one prayers with God and then to close this time with a simple "Amen."

KNOWING CHRIST

GENESIS 3:1—21

INTRODUCTION

Throughout the entire Bible there is something theologians call the "crimson thread." This is a theme from Genesis to Revelation that reveals the central place of blood in God's plan to forgive His people of their sins. In this session you will look at four key places where this theme is clearly portrayed. These are only a sampling of over 350 references to blood in the Bible. When you pair this with almost 300 uses of the word sacrifice, there is no denying the central place of blood sacrifice in the Bible.

All of this imagery in the Old Testament points to the final sacrifice for sin, Jesus Christ. In this first session you will look clearly at the very core of the Christian faith. If we miss this, nothing else will make sense.

THE BIG PICTURE

Take time to read this introduction with the group. There are suggestions for how this can be done in the beginning of the leader's section.

A WIDE ANGLE VIEW

Question One Responses to this question could range from very serious and spiritual to very light. Encourage freedom and be aware that things could go very deep quickly. If this happens, as a leader seek to sense where the Spirit is leading.

A BIBLICAL PORTRAIT

Read Genesis 3:1–21

Question Two At the very beginning of time God was in perfect fellowship with Adam and Eve. He gave them only one boundary: Do not eat the fruit of one specific tree in the garden. He told them that if they ate this fruit, they would die.

God had given Adam and Eve free will, and this commandment was to be the acid test of how they would exercise that freedom. Would they agree with the commands of God or would they take it upon themselves to disobey God and suffer the consequences?

Adam and Eve had no need to eat of that tree. Everything they needed was provided for them. However, tempted by the devil in the form of a serpent, they both ate of the tree. The minute they did, they gazed upon each other and became embarrassed, realizing they were naked. We read in the text that they sewed fig leaves together to put around themselves.

Not only were Adam and Eve uncomfortable with one another's gaze, but we read that something changed in their relationship with God. When God came into the garden they were uncomfortable because they felt His gaze as well. They hid themselves in the dense foliage. God had to ask, "Where are you? Why are you hiding from Me? Have you eaten from the tree?" Adam and Eve hemmed and hawed, and blamed one another and the serpent. Clearly, their relationship with God had changed.

Question Three When Adam and Eve sinned, God cursed the serpent, He cursed the ground, and He made man and woman painfully aware of the consequences of their sin. In other words, He said that people would live with the residual effects of Adam and Eve's disobedience from that day on. Throughout history people would live in a sin-infested society. There would be disease, death, labor in growing crops, and pain in childbirth. Adam and Eve hung their heads in shame.

Before God left Adam and Eve that day He did something that many people miss. We read that God looked at their fig leaves and knew they were not sufficient for covering their shame so He found an animal and slaughtered it. The Creator of the universe skinned the animal and used those skins to put around Adam and Eve. Now, Adam and Eve didn't know anything about death. They had never seen blood flow. They had never heard an animal cry out in pain as it was being slaughtered. They had never seen the unsightly view of a crumpled corpse as its blood soaked into the ground. I can only imagine that they gasped in horror as they now witnessed God identifying an innocent third party and slaughtering it. Blood flowed that God might cover their nakedness.

You can bet for as long as Adam and Eve wore that skin, they were reminded that sin is a very, very serious thing. Sin is serious because it is a violation of the holiness of God. The Bible says that the wages of sin is death. God extended grace to

Adam and Eve, but they learned a lesson in the killing of an innocent animal for their sins.

SHARPENING THE FOCUS

Read Snapshot "The Passover Lamb" before Question 4

Questions Four & Five Can you imagine what went on in those moments as the father slaughtered the sheep? The boy undoubtedly turned his head away, not wanting to hear the bleating of that sheep as it was slaughtered. The father then took a basin and filled it with the blood, and placed the blood on the doorpost of the house. What a powerful image!

This story might be familiar to some in your group. Not only is it recorded clearly in the book of Exodus, but it has been made into a movie many people have seen. The story of the judgment of God on Egypt becomes personal when we look at it through the eyes of this father and son. Once again, an innocent third party would pay the price, this time to save the lives of the firstborn sons of the people of Israel.

Read Snapshot "A Perfect Sacrifice Is Coming" before Question 6

Question Six Isaiah points clearly to the coming of Jesus. When we look back from our vantage point, we can see how the person Isaiah is prophesying about is Jesus. Take time as a group to talk about the promises of this passage. Encourage group members to personalize their response. Do not have them answer what Jesus would do someday; have them focus on what Isaiah promised Jesus would do for them!

Question Seven Now you have looked at three sections of this crimson thread: the blood shed in the garden to provide covering for Adam and Eve, the Passover lamb of Exodus, and the prophecy of Jesus' sacrificial death. Take time as a group and begin to tie these Old Testament themes to Jesus. Draw parallels between the sacrificial lamb of Israel and the person of Jesus.

It is critical to see the clear connection between the sacrifices of the Old Testament and the person of Jesus. Without this connection, the death of Jesus does not make as much sense.

Read Snapshot "Jesus, the Final Sacrifice" before Question 8

Question Eight Some people think that because Jesus died for the sins of the world, everyone in the world has their sins forgiven and can plan on spending eternity in heaven. Not true! Go back to the Exodus story we studied in this session. God said He was going to pour out judgment on all the households except those who had their doorways sprinkled with blood. Those who didn't sprinkle the doorway of their home woke up to a harsh reality—a member of their family was dead.

People can sit in church every single week and agree with the theology. They can believe that God is holy and that sin must be paid for—even that sin must be paid for by an innocent third party. But until an individual applies the blood of Jesus Christ to the doorway of the heart, he or she is lost. It has to be a personal decision, a humble turning from any hope of saving self and a complete trust in Christ for cleansing and forgiveness.

Take time to discuss at what point group members made this commitment to accept Jesus. Also, allow anyone who has not made this life-changing commitment to pray and ask for the blood of Jesus to be applied to the doorway of his or her heart.

PUTTING YOURSELF IN THE PICTURE

Let the group members know you will be providing time at the beginning of the next meeting for them to discuss how they have put their faith into action. Let them tell about how they have acted on one of the two options above. However, don't limit their interaction to these two options. They may have put themselves into the picture in some other way as a result of your study.

Allow for honest and open communication. Also, be clear that there will not be any kind of a "test" or forced reporting. All you are going to do is allow time for people to volunteer to talk about how they have applied what they learned in your last study. Some group members will feel pressured if they think you are going to make everyone report on how they acted on these action goals. You don't want anyone to skip the next group because they are afraid of having to say they did not follow up on what they learned from the prior session. The key is to provide a place for honest communication without creating pressure and fear of being embarrassed.

Every session from this point on will open with a look back at the "Putting Yourself in the Picture" section of the previous session.

LIVING WITH ASSURANCE

LUKE 16:19—31

INTRODUCTION

There are many people inside and outside churches who
believe they will be going to heaven but who will not be
going. This may seem like a harsh statement, but Jesus was
clear that not everyone who claimed to know Him was really
His follower. Listen to the words of Jesus: "Not everyone who
says to me, 'Lord, Lord,' will enter the kingdom of heaven,
but only he who does the will of my Father who is in heaven.
Many will say to me on that day, 'Lord, Lord, did we not
prophesy in your name, and in your name drive out demons
and perform many miracles?' Then I will tell them plainly, 'I
never knew you. Away from me, you evildoers!'" (Matt.
7:21–23). In this session we will seek to clarify how a person
can be certain he or she is a follower of Christ.

THE BIG PICTURE

Take time to read this introduction with the group. There are
suggestions for how this can be done in the beginning of the
leader's section.

A WIDE ANGLE VIEW

Question One Many people are planning on gaining entrance
into the kingdom of heaven because they are "pretty decent"
people. The real question is, decent compared to whom? The
standard of the holiness of God is the only one against which
we will be measured. In light of God's perfection, none of us
measures up. Still, we play the comparison game in almost
every area of life. Somehow we have this sense that God will
be grading on a curve and that, since there are plenty of people
worse than us, we will probably pass the test.

A BIBLICAL PORTRAIT

Read Luke 16:19–31

Questions Two & Three The Bible is the only authoritative truth source that says something conclusive about the life hereafter. It says that there are two places people will spend eternity: a real heaven, which has been created for people to live in God's presence forever and ever, and a real hell, which has been created for people to spend eternity apart from God in condemnation and punishment. We are all going to be in one of those two places when this life ends.

If you have group members who are not sure about where they will spend eternity, it is time to face this important issue. The problem with today's existential society is that everyone lives for the moment. Many people lead their lives as if they will never die: "Other people go into the life beyond. I don't." The truth is, we will all face eternity. We need to face the hard reality that heaven or hell awaits every man, woman, and child who walks the face of this earth.

SHARPENING THE FOCUS

Read Snapshot "How Good Is Good Enough?" before Question 4

Questions Four & Five This is a very common response from those who do not follow Christ. They are playing the comparison game and hoping their good works measure up. When faced with such a response, it might help to explain the difference between religion and Christianity. This is explained very clearly in the book *Becoming a Contagious Christian*. Here is a brief overview:

Religion is spelled D-O. It is all about what we do. I go to church, I help people, I live a good life, I believe certain things, and the list goes on and on. Christianity is spelled D-O-N-E. It is all about what God has done for us. God gave His Son as the sacrifice for our sins, He reached out to us, He paid the price, and the way to heaven was opened by His loving generosity. As a matter of fact, when Jesus was dying on the cross, He said, "It is finished!" This was His way of saying He had paid the price for all our sins. The bottom line is clear: None of us can earn our way into heaven by anything we do. God has opened the way through Christ and we can accept His gift.

As it says in Ephesians 2:8–9, "For it is by grace you have been saved, through faith—and this not from yourselves, it is the gift of God—not by works, so that no one can boast."

Read Snapshot "False Assurances" before Question 6

Questions Six & Seven Some people say, "I am a Christian because I believe in God and say my prayers." But this is not enough. According to James 2:19, even the demons believe in God and tremble! The truth is, a set of doctrines never opened heaven to anyone.

This is like a person who asserts, "I correspond regularly with the President of our country." What does this mean? If it means this person writes letters to the White House on a regular basis, big deal. It's only a big deal if the President writes back personally. You can say you believe in the concept of God and that you say your prayers, but does God respond to your prayers? Does God say, "That's my son! That's my daughter!" Or does He say, "Who are you? I don't know you."

Some people claim to be Christians because they attend church. You can have perfect church attendance for the rest of your life and still end up with a bogus ticket. Attending a session of the U.S. Congress doesn't make you a senator. Attending the Olympics will not make you an Olympic-class athlete. In the same way, attending church does not necessarily make you a Christian.

There are many people who say, "I am a Christian because I was baptized." Have you ever heard that one? There is not one place in Scripture that guarantees salvation through the sacrament of baptism. As precious and needful as baptism is, the water of baptism never cleansed anyone of their sin.

Read Snapshot "Five Biblical Convictions" before Question 8

Question Eight Not every follower of Christ can give a day and hour when they became a Christian. However, most can identify a season of life where their faith became real. Invite group members to communicate this point of change and celebrate what God has done in their life. For those who have not yet responded to Christ's offer of forgiveness, this will be a great chance for them to hear the many and varied ways God brings people to Himself.

PUTTING YOURSELF IN THE PICTURE

Challenge group members to take time in the coming week to use part or all of this application section as an opportunity for continued growth.

Keys to Spiritual Growth

Acts 2:38—47

Introduction

In this session we will look at four critical elements of growth for all followers of Christ. First, God's Word says if we are ever going to mature, we need the transforming teaching of the Scriptures. We need to be in a church where the Word of God is taught with power and we are encouraged to apply it to our lives. Second, we need fellowship. We need to build strong relationships with brothers and sisters who are fully devoted followers of Christ.

Third, communion is essential for Christian growth. We need to gather with God's people and partake in the sacrament of the Lord's Supper. This regular reminder of God's love deepens our faith. And fourth, we need to learn how to pour our heart out to God in prayer.

The Big Picture

Take time to read this introduction with the group. There are suggestions for how this can be done in the beginning of the leader's section.

A Wide Angle View

Question One Every Christ follower desires to grow in their faith. Sometimes we sense that we are experiencing a growth spurt; at other times we feel like we are going through a desert time of dryness. Invite group members to communicate how they have been experiencing growth over the past year.

A Biblical Portrait

Read Acts 2:38–47

Questions Two & Three A fully devoted follower of Christ will experience transformation. It may not come overnight, but it will come! Such transformation is God's plan for our lives.

Ephesians 4:23 teaches that our thoughts and attitudes must constantly be changing for the better. Second Corinthians 5:17 says that Christ helps us become a whole new person. As Christians we discover new ethics, values, relationships, vocabulary, ambitions, personality traits, dreams, and so much more. When we commit to follow Christ personally, we will crave spiritual growth. It will become one of the highest priorities in our life.

In the second chapter of Acts we see a portrait of the early church. These Christ followers hungered for growth and committed themselves to God and each other. Take time as a group to look at the attitudes and actions of the early Christians. How does that early community of faith compare to the Christian community you see today?

Sharpening the Focus

Read Snapshot "Devoted to Learning" before Question 4

Questions Four & Five The early Christians devoted themselves to the teaching of God's Word. They recognized the need to hear God's truth taught on a regular basis. We too need to find teachers who God can use to feed us and challenge us in our faith. We need to devote ourselves to attend church regularly, come prepared to listen, take time to analyze and interact with the truth that is presented, and devote ourselves to the application of what we hear. It is critical for every Christian to be in a church where they can sit under the teaching of someone who really feeds them.

Read Snapshot "Committed to Fellowship" before Question 6

Question Six We live in a day of Lone Rangers. Too many followers of Christ seem to try to follow Him alone. God made us for community. When we try to stand alone in our faith, we are resisting His plan for our lives. When I make hospital visits, I can usually identify those Christ followers who resist fellowship and those who embrace it. Those who are part of a small group, who are in deep community with others and serve God hand-in-hand with a team of people, have flowers on the shelf, cards posted all over the wall, and visitors lining up at the door. Those who have decided to walk alone often suffer alone. It is a sad but true reality. We need to commit ourselves to investing in the lives of others and be willing to let them get close enough to enter into our joy and our pain.

**Read Snapshot "A Hunger for Communion"
before Question 7**

Question Seven Communion is one of the deepest and most powerful reminders of the love and the sacrifice God made so that we could become His followers. Many of your group members who have experienced communion will be able to describe times God has touched them deeply during this time. Allow an open forum for them to describe how God has spoken to them, met them, and transformed them through this powerful time of remembering the sacrifice of Christ.

**Read Snapshot "A Passion for Prayer"
before Question 8**

Question Eight We all have things that can distract us and stand in the way of deep communication with God. There are also those things that create an atmosphere conducive to prayer. Compare notes as a small group and discover how you can grow in prayer.

Question Nine Take time to communicate areas in which you need prayer support from group members. You may want to close your group with a time of praying for one another.

PUTTING YOURSELF IN THE PICTURE

Challenge group members to take time in the coming week to use part or all of this application section as an opportunity for continued growth.

GETTING UP AFTER FALLING DOWN

PSALM 1

INTRODUCTION

The question is not, "Will I ever fall?" The question for every follow of Christ is, "When I do fall, what will I do?" The enemy wants us to get discouraged and stay on the ground. God wants us to learn how to keep getting up after we fall down. This session will focus on how we can do two things: first, how we can do everything possible to keep from falling; second, how we can get back up when we do fall. God's desire is for His followers to fall less and less as the years pass. However, no matter how long a person has been a Christian and no matter how devoted that person is in his or her faith, there will still be times when we stumble and fall. At these times we need to get up and keep moving forward.

THE BIG PICTURE

Take time to read this introduction with the group. There are suggestions for how this can be done in the beginning of the leader's section.

A WIDE ANGLE VIEW

Question One For most of us, not a day passes that we don't say yes and no to God. Take time with your group to tell different group members' stories. The stories where people said yes to God will be a celebration of how the Holy Spirit is moving in the lives of your group members. The responses to the second part of the question could move in many directions. There could be very safe responses, such as "I knew I shouldn't have had that extra slice of pie," or very serious responses, such as "I destroyed my marriage because I was unfaithful to my wife." The key is to identify that all of us face the choice of saying yes and no to God every day.

A BIBLICAL PORTRAIT

Read Psalm 1

Questions Two & Three Psalm 1 is a perfect illustration of where both the "yes" and "no" paths lead. The illustration shows two guys on very different life-tracks. One guy has developed a track record of saying yes to God; the other has developed a track record of saying no to God.

One guy's delight is in the law of the Lord. In that law, in the Word of God, he meditates day and night. He likes saying yes to God. Whatever God says he responds, "Yes, count me in. I am going to go that way." What happens to that man? The psalmist says he will be like a tree firmly planted by the streams of water. In other words, he is going to have a life of strength and stability. His life will be like a fruitful tree with deep roots. He is going to have a productive life. Whatever he does he will prosper. There is going to be a vitality, a creativity that is not his own, a zest for life that defies human logic. This is what happens to people who say yes to God!

Now let's look at the guy who says no to God. What lies down that path? This man is like the leaves we see blowing in the wind with no direction. His life will spin out of control. He will have no vision, no direction, no sense of rootedness. He will start hiding from other Christians, feeling guilty and ashamed. He won't go near a church. It is a sad and tragic picture, but it does reflect the life of many people.

SHARPENING THE FOCUS

Read Snapshot "Never Say No to God" before Question 4

Question Four You are now four sessions into this small group study. This question will be a hinge point for your group. In the first question of this session you asked group members to talk about a time they said yes or no in the past. This is a great deal easier than talking about what we are facing now. Invite group members to express one area where they are being tempted to say no to God.

As a group, commit to pray for one another. Allow a place for accountability in the coming weeks of your group. If people are willing to be honest about where they are facing temptation to disobey God, this will open a place for mutual support and accountability that will move your group to a deeper level.

**Read Snapshot "Say Yes to God's Word"
before Question 5**

Questions Five & Six Saying yes to God is not a simple, one-time decision. In some areas of life we need to say yes every single day. Take time as a group to focus on the areas in which you are feeling led to say yes to God. Where are you in the process? How can you encourage and support each other?

**Read Snapshot "Take Your Sins to Jesus"
before Question 7**

Question Seven When you fall, confess your sins and get back up. Claim God's forgiveness. Hide it in your heart. Realize that God has amnesia over your sin. Your sins have been separated from you as far as the east is from the west. That is a long way! God loves you so much that He forgives you. Silence the voice of the accuser with the Word of God. Declare it: "I have been forgiven through the death of Jesus. His blood paid the price and I am free!" Live with this confidence.

**Read Snapshot "Confess Your Sins to Each Other"
before Question 8**

Questions Eight & Nine The practice of confession is as old as the Christian church; however, it is foreign to many Christ followers. We live in an individualistic society where we often take an "it's no one else's business" attitude. As a matter of fact, we spend a great deal of energy and time covering up our mistakes and doing all we can to be sure no one sees our sin. Now God says, "Confess your sins to each other." Wow! This is counter-cultural and radical. It goes against every fiber in our being.

Confession creates a place for accountability and support like nothing else does. As a group, seek to create a place and climate where confession can happen and mutual support can grow through the experience of confession.

PUTTING YOURSELF IN THE PICTURE

Challenge group members to take time in the coming week to use part or all of this application section as an opportunity for continued growth.

BEING CHRISTIAN IN A NON-CHRISTIAN WORLD

MATTHEW 5:13–16

INTRODUCTION

One of the worst diseases in Christendom today is isolationism. We get hurt because of some ridicule or rejection from the world, so we run into a closet and close the door. Inside the darkness of that enclosed space we say, "I know what the plan is now. I am going to find a nice church, some nice Christian friends, join a nice small group and play it safe. No more venturing out into the dangers of the world for me! Maybe other people can take the kind of hurt I just felt, but I can't. I am going to find a holy huddle and stand in the middle of it."

Most of your group members have had those feelings at one time or another. What we discover as we follow Christ is that we must learn to die to ourselves and also to the opinions of others. We can't be fully devoted followers of Christ and still be consumed with what everyone else thinks about us. In this session we will focus on how we can be Christians in a world that will often criticize us for doing what is right in God's sight.

We need to learn how to let our light shine and how to be salt in the world.

THE BIG PICTURE

Take time to read this introduction with the group. There are suggestions for how this can be done in the beginning of the leader's section.

A WIDE ANGLE VIEW

Question One When we realize all we have in Christ, we are motivated to share what we have with others. The responses we can receive are many and varied. Sometimes people are very open, but at other times they are very resistant. Take time as a group to give a few of the possible endings to this story. In the midst of this discussion you may hear people telling their own story of how someone responded to them when they had the courage to communicate their faith.

A Biblical Portrait

Read Matthew 5:13–16

Questions Two & Three Think about salt for a moment and why Jesus chose to use salt as a metaphor for how Christians should go out and affect the world. What does salt do? One obvious answer is that it makes you thirsty. Isn't that why it is widely served in bars? Bar owners want people to eat salty pretzels, peanuts, or popcorn so they will drink more beverages. Salt makes people thirsty.

Salt also spices things up a bit. Can you imagine corn-on-the-cob without salt? It enhances the flavor. Many foods would be bland without a dash of salt to bring out the flavor.

Salt also preserves. Long before the days of the refrigerator, salt was used to keep certain foods from spoiling. Certain meats could be preserved for long periods of time if they were packed in salt.

So salt creates thirst, enhances flavor, and preserves. This leads us to the big question: What specifically did Jesus have in mind when He looked at His followers and said, "You are the salt of the earth"? We don't know for certain. Maybe Jesus meant for the metaphor of salt to symbolize all three.

Jesus also calls Christians to be light in this world of darkness. Light illuminates dark places and helps us see where we need to go. It takes away fear and allows us to move ahead with confidence. When we decide to let our lives shine before the world, we naturally reflect this light to those around us. As God's light-bearers, we need to be sure nothing keeps His light from shining in our lives. As a matter of fact, we are called to be sure the light continues to shine brightly.

Take time as a group to define what letting our light shine means in the context of Jesus' teaching and our lives.

Sharpening the Focus

**Read Snapshot "Secret Ambassadors"
before Question 4**

Questions Four & Five Many people in the church function as secret ambassadors. They are closet Christians, changing with their surroundings. They come to church and fit in with everyone else, but on Monday morning they head back into the marketplace, neighborhood, or schools and become a different person. Their secret motto is, "When in Rome, do as the Romans do."

Take time as a group to identify some of the elements of what this kind of ambassador looks like. Also, seek to clarify some of the possible consequences of living with this approach to the Christian life.

Read Snapshot "Obnoxious Ambassadors" before Question 6

Question Six Most of us have been accosted by obnoxious ambassadors. We know how offensive it can be to be "gunned down" with their faith. Take time to tell some war stories and encourage group members to never treat anyone like this.

Question Seven There is a great deal of room between these two extremes. We can't hide our faith and cover up our light, nor can we shine our light into people's eyes and blind them. We need to strike a healthy balance. Take time as a group to discuss the middle ground of balance between these two poles.

Read Snapshot "Spirit-Led Ambassadors" before Question 8

Question Eight Now that you have been introduced to these three types of ambassadors, choose one of the scenarios given and describe how each different ambassador might respond. Identify negative scenarios and challenge people to avoid them. Then, identify positive and healthy approaches and encourage these in group members.

PUTTING YOURSELF IN THE PICTURE

Challenge group members to take time in the coming week to use part or all of this application section as an opportunity for continued growth.

GUIDANCE ALONG THE WAY

PSALM 23

INTRODUCTION

God still speaks to His people. In this session we will look at three distinct ways God speaks to His followers. If we are ready and willing to listen, God will speak through His written Word (the Bible), through the inner guidance of the Holy Spirit, and through the counsel of wise Christians. If we are going to be fully devoted followers of Christ, we will need to take advantage of each of these sources of guidance.

THE BIG PICTURE

Take time to read this introduction with the group. There are suggestions for how this can be done in the beginning of the leader's section.

A WIDE ANGLE VIEW

Question One Provide time for group members to tell their stories of being lost. The need for help and guidance will come through clearly in many of these stories.

A BIBLICAL PORTRAIT

Read Psalm 23

Questions Two & Three This may be one of the most familiar passages in the Bible. Even many nonbelievers have heard it read. Take time as a group to read this psalm and talk about its various promises of guidance and provision. Each of these promises is drawn from the image of a shepherd and his flock as well as of the Lord and His people. Seek to clarify these parallels as you look at the passage. Also, take time to unpack all you can learn about the heart of God from this psalm. He has the heart of a shepherd; He desires to protect us and provide for us.

SHARPENING THE FOCUS

Read Snapshot "Guidance from the Bible" before Question 4

Question Four This question deals with a couple of common statements non-Christians make about the Bible. Our response to them is very important. Defensiveness and frustration rarely help; we need to respond in a way that wins people over. If someone says the Bible is dry, tell them about how alive and powerful it is in your life. If they say the Bible is irrelevant, tell them about a recent time a biblical message hit home in your life.

Question Five We all need support and accountability in our lives when it comes to our commitment to grow in knowing God's Word. Take time to create an atmosphere of mutual encouragement and affirmation in this area. Encourage group members to be very specific about their goals so that there can be clear lines of accountability.

Read Snapshot "The Inner Guidance of the Holy Spirit" before Question 6

Questions Six & Seven Learning to hear the still and quiet voice of the Holy Spirit takes time. It also takes faith and courage. When a person feels a prompting, they need to learn how to act on this while still listening for greater clarity. In the Snapshot you read of a simple process that can help a person develop a listening ear for the Spirit. Allow your group members to describe how they have heard the Spirit speak. You may also want to look at the second "Putting Yourself in the Picture" exercise at the end of this session to help give more clarity on how a person can begin developing a discipline of listening.

Read Snapshot "Guidance Through Other Christ Followers" before Question 8

Questions Eight & Nine There is great wisdom in seeking counsel from other mature believers. This counsel can come from one person or from a group of people you respect. Describe how God has spoken to you through the wise counsel of other Christ followers. Clarify how your small group can function as a source of wisdom and godly counsel in your lives.

PUTTING YOURSELF IN THE PICTURE

Challenge group members to take time in the coming week to use part or all of this application section as an opportunity for continued growth.

ADDITIONAL WILLOW CREEK RESOURCES

Small Group Resources

Coaching Life-Changing Small Group Leaders, by Bill Donahue and Greg Bowman
The Complete Book of Questions, by Garry Poole
The Connecting Church, by Randy Frazee
Leading Life-Changing Small Groups, by Bill Donahue and the Willow Creek Team
The Seven Deadly Sins of Small Group Ministry, by Bill Donahue and Russ Robinson
Walking the Small Group Tightrope, by Bill Donahue and Russ Robinson

Evangelism Resources

Becoming a Contagious Christian (book), by Bill Hybels and Mark Mittelberg
The Case for a Creator, by Lee Strobel
The Case for Christ, by Lee Strobel
The Case for Faith, by Lee Strobel
Seeker Small Groups, by Garry Poole
The Three Habits of Highly Contagious Christians, by Garry Poole

Spiritual Gifts and Ministry

Network Revised (training course), by Bruce Bugbee and Don Cousins
The Volunteer Revolution, by Bill Hybels
What You Do Best in the Body of Christ—Revised, by Bruce Bugbee

Marriage and Parenting

Fit to Be Tied, by Bill and Lynne Hybels
Surviving a Spiritual Mismatch in Marriage, by Lee and Leslie Strobel

Ministry Resources

An Hour on Sunday, by Nancy Beach
Building a Church of Small Groups, by Bill Donahue and Russ Robinson
The Heart of the Artist, by Rory Noland
Making Your Children's Ministry the Best Hour of Every Kid's Week, by Sue Miller and
    David Staal
Thriving as an Artist in the Church, by Rory Noland

Curriculum

An Ordinary Day with Jesus, by John Ortberg and Ruth Haley Barton
Becoming a Contagious Christian (kit), by Mark Mittelberg, Lee Strobel, and Bill Hybels
Good Sense Budget Course, by Dick Towner, John Tofilon, and the Willow Creek Team
If You Want to Walk on Water, You've Got to Get Out of the Boat, by John Ortberg with
    Stephen and Amanda Sorenson
The Life You've Always Wanted, by John Ortberg with Stephen and Amanda Sorenson
The Old Testament Challenge, by John Ortberg with Kevin and Sherry Harney, Mindy
    Caliguire, and Judson Poling

Willow Creek Association

Vision, Training, Resources for Prevailing Churches

This resource was created to serve you and to help you build a local church that prevails. It is just one of many ministry tools that are part of the Willow Creek Resources® line, published by the Willow Creek Association together with Zondervan.

The Willow Creek Association (WCA) was created in 1992 to serve a rapidly growing number of churches from across the denominational spectrum that are committed to helping unchurched people become fully devoted followers of Christ. Membership in the WCA now numbers over 12,000 Member Churches worldwide from more than ninety denominations.

The Willow Creek Association links like-minded Christian leaders with each other and with strategic vision, training, and resources in order to help them build prevailing churches designed to reach their redemptive potential. Here are some of the ways the WCA does that.

- **The Leadership Summit**—a once a year, two-and-a-half-day conference to envision and equip Christians with leadership gifts and responsibilities. Presented live at Willow Creek as well as via satellite broadcast to over 130 locations across North America, this event is designed to increase the leadership effectiveness of pastors, ministry staff, volunteer church leaders, and Christians in the marketplace.

- **Ministry-Specific Conferences** — throughout each year the WCA hosts a variety of conferences and training events — both at Willow Creek's main campus and offsite, across the U.S., and around the world — targeting church leaders and volunteers in ministry-specific areas such as: small groups, preaching and teaching, the arts, children, students, volunteers, stewardship, etc.

- **Willow Creek Resources®** — provides churches with trusted and field-tested ministry resources in such areas as leadership, evangelism, spiritual formation, spiritual gifts, small groups, stewardship, student ministry, children's ministry, the use of the arts — drama, media, contemporary music — and more.

- **WCA Member Benefits** — includes substantial discounts to WCA training events, a 20 percent discount on all Willow Creek Resources®, *Defining Moments* monthly audio journal for leaders, quarterly *Willow* magazine, access to a Members-Only section on WillowNet, monthly communications, and more. Member Churches also receive special discounts and premier services through WCA's growing number of ministry partners — Select Service Providers — and save an average of $500 annually depending on the level of engagement.

For specific information about WCA conferences, resources, membership, and other ministry services contact:

Willow Creek Association
P.O. Box 3188
Barrington, IL 60011-3188
Phone: 847-570-9812
Fax: 847-765-5046
www.willowcreek.com

Continue building your new community!
New Community Series
BILL HYBELS AND JOHN ORTBERG
with Kevin and Sherry Harney

Exodus: *Journey Toward God* 978-0-310-22771-7

Parables: *Imagine Life God's Way* 978-0-310-22881-3

Sermon on the Mount¹: *Connect with God* 978-0-310-22883-7

Sermon on the Mount²: *Connect with Others* 978-0-310-22884-4

Acts: *Build Community* 978-0-310-22770-0

Romans: *Find Freedom* 978-0-310-22765-6

Philippians: *Run the Race* 978-0-310-3314-5

Colossians: *Discover the New You* 978-0-310-22769-4

James: *Live Wisely* 978-0-310-22767-0

1 Peter: *Stand Strong* 978-0-310-22773-1

1 John: *Love Each Other* 978-0-310-22768-7

Revelation: *Experience God's Power* 978-0-310-22882-0

Look for New Community at your local Christian bookstore.

Continue the Transformation
Pursuing Spiritual Transformation
JOHN ORTBERG, LAURIE PEDERSON,
AND JUDSON POLING

Grace: *An Invitation to a Way of Life* 978-0-310-22074-9

Growth: *Training vs. Trying* 978-0-310-22075-6

Groups: *The Life-Giving Power of Community* 978-0-310-22076-3

Gifts: *The Joy of Serving God* 978-0-310-22077-0

Giving: *Unlocking the Heart of Good Stewardship* 978-0-310-22078-7

Fully Devoted: *Living Each Day in Jesus' Name* 978-0-310-22073-2

Look for Pursuing Spiritual Transformation at your local Christian bookstore.

TOUGH QUESTIONS
Garry Poole and Judson Poling

Softcover

How Does Anyone Know God Exists?	ISBN 978-0-310-24502-5
What Difference Does Jesus Make?	ISBN 978-0-310-24503-2
How Reliable Is the Bible?	ISBN 978-0-310-24504-9
How Could God Allow Suffering and Evil?	ISBN 978-0-310-24505-6
Don't All Religions Lead to God?	ISBN 978-0-310-24506-3
Do Science and the Bible Conflict?	ISBN 978-0-310-24507-0
Why Become a Christian?	ISBN 978-0-310-24508-7
Leader's Guide	ISBN 978-0-310-24509-4

REALITY CHECK SERIES
by Mark Ashton

Winning at Life	ISBN: 978-0-310-24525-4
Leadership Jesus Style	ISBN: 978-0-310-24526-1
When Tragedy Strikes	ISBN: 978-0-310-24524-7
Sudden Impact	ISBN: 978-0-310-24522-3
Jesus' Greatest Moments	ISBN: 978-0-310-24528-5
Hot Issues	ISBN: 978-0-310-24523-0
Future Shock	ISBN: 978-0-310-24527-8
Clear Evidence	ISBN: 978-0-310-24746-3

An Ordinary Day with Jesus

*Experiencing the Reality
of God in Your Everyday Life*

This 8-session, ready-to-teach curriculum guides and equips both leaders and participants in concrete ways to embrace the very real person of Jesus Christ in everyday life

Take the first steps toward that kind of life today. *An Ordinary Day with Jesus* is designed to show you how. The practices and teaching detailed here can literally change your life, one ordinary-extraordinary-day at a time. Experiencing God's presence in your everyday life doesn't necessarily mean doing new things. It means doing the things you already do in new ways—with him. An ordinary day with Jesus truly can be the greatest day you've ever had. Best of all, it can lead to an extraordinary life!

The complete kit includes:
- Leader's Guide
- Participant's Guide
- 45-minute video cassette
- PowerPoint® CD-ROM

Kit
ISBN: 978-0-310-24587-2
VHS Video
ISBN: 978-0-310-24557-5
Leader's Guide
ISBN: 978-0-310-24585-8
Participant's Guide
ISBN: 978-0-310-24586-5

Pick up a copy today at your favorite bookstore!

God Is Closer Than You Think

This Can Be the Greatest Moment of Your Life Because This Moment Is the Place Where You Can Meet God

John Ortberg

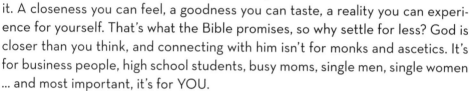

What Are You Waiting For?

Intimacy with God can happen right now if you want it. A closeness you can feel, a goodness you can taste, a reality you can experience for yourself. That's what the Bible promises, so why settle for less? God is closer than you think, and connecting with him isn't for monks and ascetics. It's for business people, high school students, busy moms, single men, single women ... and most important, it's for YOU.

God Is Closer Than You Think shows how you can enjoy a vibrant, moment-by-moment relationship with your heavenly Father. Bestselling author John Ortberg reveals the face of God waiting to be discovered in the complex mosaic of your life. He shows you God's hand stretching toward you. And, with his gift for storytelling, Ortberg illustrates the ways you can reach toward God and complete the connection—to your joy and his.

Hardcover, Jacketed: 978-0-310-25349-5
Unabridged Audio CD: 978-0-310-26379-1
Curriculum Kit: 978-0-310-26635-8
DVD: 978-0-310-26637-2
Participant's Guide: 978-0-310-26639-6
Audio Download, Unabridged: 978-0-310-26700-3

ebooks:
Adobe® Acrobat® eBook Reader®: 978-0-310-26336-4
Microsoft Reader®: 978-0-310-26337-1
Palm™ Reader: 978-0-310-26338-8
Mobipocket Reader™: 978-0-310-26339-5

Pick up a copy today at your favorite bookstore!

An Hour on Sunday

Creating Moments of Transformation and Wonder

Nancy Beach

Today's spiritually searching culture is less inclined than ever to attend church. Yet, no time of the week is filled with more life-changing potential than Sunday morning.

Imagine . . .

- experiences that bring people heart-to-heart with God.
- messages in which God's truth connects to everyday life.
- transcendent moments that leave people awestruck—and transformed.

That's what can happen when you unleash the arts in your church through the power of the Holy Spirit. *An Hour on Sunday* is not about nitty-gritty programming details or cookie-cutter how-to's. It's about foundational issues—ten enduring principles that:

- unite artists and ministry leaders around a common language
- empower artists and pastors to effectively work together, and
- create the potential for moments that matter on Sunday morning.

An Hour on Sunday is for worship and arts ministry leaders, pastors and teachers, artists—including musicians, writers, dancers, actors, visual artists, film makers, light and sound engineers—and anyone who believes in the limitless potential of the arts in their church.

Whimsically illustrated, written with passion and humor, and filled with stories of both success and failure, *An Hour on Sunday* explores the deep, shaping forces that can make your hour on Sunday a time of transformation and wonder for believers and seekers alike.

Jacketed Hardcover: 978-0-310-25296-2

Pick up a copy today at your favorite bookstore!

The Case for Christ

A Journalist's
Personal Investigation
of the Evidence for Jesus

Lee Strobel

Using the dramatic scenario of an investigative journalist pursuing a story, Lee Strobel uses his experience as a reporter for the *Chicago Tribune* to interview experts about the evidence for Christ from the fields of science, philosophy, and history. Winner of the Gold Medallion Book Award and twice nominated for the Christian Book of the Year Award.

Hardcover: 978-0-310-22646-8

The Case for Faith

A Journalist Investigates
the Toughest Objections
to Christianity

Lee Strobel

This eagerly anticipated sequel to Lee Strobel's bestselling *Case for Christ* finds the author investigating the nettlesome issues and doubts of the heart that threaten faith. Eight major topics are addressed, including doubt, the problem of pain, and the existence of evil.

Hardcover: 978-0-310-22015-2

Share Your Thoughts

With the Author: Your comments will be forwarded to the author when you send them to *zauthor@zondervan.com*.

With Zondervan: Submit your review of this book by writing to *zreview@zondervan.com*.

Free Online Resources at
www.zondervan.com/hello

 Zondervan AuthorTracker: Be notified whenever your favorite authors publish new books, go on tour, or post an update about what's happening in their lives.

 Daily Bible Verses and Devotions: Enrich your life with daily Bible verses or devotions that help you start every morning focused on God.

 Free Email Publications: Sign up for newsletters on fiction, Christian living, church ministry, parenting, and more.

 Zondervan Bible Search: Find and compare Bible passages in a variety of translations at www.zondervanbiblesearch.com.

 Other Benefits: Register yourself to receive online benefits like coupons and special offers, or to participate in research.